THE NATION'S SADDEST LOVE POEMS

Paranormal investigator & erotic doomsday prophet, **Sam J. Grudgings** (he/him) is a queer poet from Bristol shortlisted for the Outspoken Poetry Prize 2020. His work explores rehabilitation via the lens of body horror, the 1920's burlesque scene & the new weird movement. Commonly found yelling poems at punk shows, his debut collection *The Bible II* investigating addiction, loss and the masculine urge to fight or fuck god, is available from Verve Poetry Press.

Also by Sam J. Grudgings

The Bible II   (Verve Poetry Press, 2021)

The Nation's Saddest Love Poems

Sam J. Grudgings

Broken Sleep Books

ISBN: 978-1-915760-94-4

Cover designed by Aaron Kent

Edited and typeset by Aaron Kent

Broken Sleep Books Ltd
Rhydwen
Talgarreg
Ceredigion
SA44 4HB

Broken Sleep Books Ltd
Fair View
St Georges Road
Cornwall
PL26 7YH

Contents

Wounds Are Rivers

Man split from tarmac tongue to standing water of his stomach
becomes flood. All this needs to be true
    is to look to your fingers, the desperately left portraits
    in riverbanks identifying the way you held on.
        If you take the drink from the man who's been taken
    by drink how long will it be till he makes it back?
        You spent too long relearning the art of seeming
    that when someone asks a simple question it isn't easy
            to answer. Instead, you pull a torrent
            of handkerchiefs from your mouth,
        gesture to an unseen audience -
        one made up of the sediment and
  jetsam and undertow - and
reveal your excuse was carefully prepared,
waiting in their top breast pocket this entire time. The river remains
unimpressed by your prestidigitation and
    commitment to remaining unknown.
        It recognises itself and
    knows it can never cross you twice.
        Haven't you had enough of being
    unfound? Don't smoke screens take their tax on your lungs?
You who have flooded time and time again cannot
    possibly have the stamina to outlast yourself.
        No one can. How churlish of an audience
        to claim that you were the trick and
    that they had seen the strings. Do they not know
    that all you are without the river is a man grieving
the ghosts he could never be. Do they not know
    that the showing of the strings

is the illusion? The real part is
in the knowing, the real part
is in the erosion, the real part
is in what's left behind. You forget,
that just because starlings arrive
with the horizon doesn't mean they bring it.
From the back waters
of your sleeve you pull a tributary,
an egress, an oxbow lake of
stagnant identities that had the better of you
when you were better off.
A jury of wild swimmers can float in the slick skin of a boy
who disappeared into water's rushing congress and
still deny the boy was water and
revel in the shallow's nostalgic apathy and
insist they knew better. How not to swim on
a stomach empty of need and
yet - as you loop through the prestige of finally finding a place to drown
- it turns out all the detritivores in the stomach of you and
the artefacts left by the tide and,
the driftwood and
the invasive species of the rivers
have named themselves *you* and even you
can't tell where it began.

Errors of the Human Body

November 2006 & there is rabbit hole ridden scrubland
in place of your formerly human body.   A diagnosis is an omen.
You are learning what it is to be precocial.   The diseases of
lagomorphs are well documented, psychopomps   of prophecy
that they are. They die in spirals. Hurrying to convey   the weight
of their lesions to crowds.   Some tumours contain teeth - dying
a smile in the bruise dark of a bodies fading   Some futures are a given. A body
is a no-dimensional idea until it is observed,   at which point it falls
victim to mortality. Your god is a callous remnant of the unrequited plea
to escape gravity. Skin sloughs from bodies & walks its own path.
A warren of names sheds the colony of holes.   Call this freedom
if you must. Raw is the body with empty. Pink is the flesh, vulnerable
to scrubland, root systems are addicted to holding the mantle of the body
together. To them it is living.   We allow microclimates to broker cauls
& wildfire across the faces   of new-borns. Birthing is the price
for knowing. A body can be born with a body already growing inside.
Actions have biomass. There is a stream trickling from the incision in the
rabbit body that will nurture the land.   The rabbit must die to achieve
its purpose.   To become a river is no   bad thing.
To become human, one must give the Spring its due.   An absence cauterised in
place of belief is a puzzle. Lucky rabbit paw you, lame of your own too much.
      Stertor rapture. Call this escape if you must. Culling season leaving
its long red of wrecking ecosystems for the stars. The body   is a source.
The body is heralding all anaemic puzzles that challenge it.   Wracking
its skin of fathom & biome, refusing to be so displaced by name.

Désordre C'est Moi

With shadows appropriating the ground long before landing, the disembodied are still laying claim to being lost. Feigning allergies to touch & coveting glitter left by wounds is a survival technique. There's plenty of ugly in the depiction of our celestial crashing - not least the trash fucked orbits of subtle bodies beholden to insignificance & the carpenter bees seeking thorax hives & the propolis of touch.

I can give up this illusion of freewill whenever I want. Recuperation of destructive pageantry. Rejection of knife edge diplomacy. Revisionism of situationist apathy. Whatever escape plan works best. If we seemed so in love with gravity, it is because it offered our best shot. We didn't know our throwing up a glitch of butterflies was anything other than context.

I've laboured under the impression my descent was in the tradition of breaking the sheer glass of wishing wells & expecting change & it was only in finding others fell for always wanting more did I realise I might be vulnerable to the doctrine of crash. Bereft of the hollow we so cherish. With our wasp chests wide open. we can't pretend it was the radicle of fern & tentacle erupting from my stomaching that so wrecked the idea of us but my buying us orchids & never visiting the museums we said we'd marry each other in. Did I fool us into thinking I was permanent? It's only appropriate this belief of betterment is contagious. We weren't to know how grateful I was for your refusal to carry me. How could we have been?

However a motif will occur before the pattern is recognised, a reflection will speak before the boy does & a swarm will communicate in an elaborately choreographed musical number tongue & translate the missteps. Lungs are parachutes. Pulse of swarm. Hearts are pulpy paper biomes. I'm laying waste to any notion that I had any idea what was good for me. It is only in brushing up on theory as to why boys with mirrored arms swarm the void that I find smoke-filled apiaries vacant of wanting. The Church of Honey was where we told each other it would be & I am working on unlearning the sticky cadaver worship of boys who wear their tombstones as disguises & treat gravity as a privilege.

Architect for a Slow Wound Day

1. BLUEPRINTS (BUILDING BETTER DAYS AT THE EXPENSE OF GLUE FACTORIES)

I feel your ribcage in Southampton, cultivating the sky as it does its best impression of London, I wonder if I have an answer for all that longing. Anticipation whetting appetites is of no service to those dying of thirst. I am a herd of gentrifiers priced out of their own weekend visits. I'm a ruined horse loose tourist, lost of museum exhibits & the history of us.

2. PLANNING PERMISSION (MAKING EXCUSES FROM SUBTEXT)

On arrival your hands are relics, clutching a tour of orange light to gift me. I'm praying tungsten. I'm praying nostalgic. I'm speeding prayerful. You still walk like train tracks. You still talk on the phone in the quiet carriages of Brighton's streets. You still say you have missed me, covering your mouth to laugh. Talk with your mouth half full of honesty & half full of who I wished I could be. I don't know what it looks like when someone stops loving me as I'm never there. I know how it is when they no longer do though.

3. FOUNDATIONS (IN WHICH THE SPEAKER IS A HORSE)

You notice my hooves. You request a stampede from honesty. You ask me about my way here. The recycled air & the views & what I was listening to. I list passengers' voices; the gossip of the tracks; my god, how much I loved you; the galloping rain in the flat dark of outside; & the longing - the endless, endless surround sound longing - of the night against the window. I want to fall asleep running headfirst into walls. I say I want to fall asleep & dream of never leaving. I want to fall into something unfamiliar & worship the symmetry of forms stuck in my throat from the pathways of light left by trains.

4. BRIBING THE GROUND FOR ALL THAT REMOVAL WORK

You claim the city is your body. Throw your orchard arms around me. Ask, *do you like what I've done with the place?* pointing to the graffiti & the gentrification. Pointing delicate to the parts of you missing that you had begged me to bring with me. We rearrange any distance. We tell ourselves we're ugly in the right wine light but never doubt the taste of each other.

5. CONSTRUCTION (IN WHICH THE INTENDED AUDIENCE IS A HOME)

Even in smiling I can see the winter of odd churches lingering. Gravity yards. Railway sidings. Locomotive beliefs. You're politer than you need to be. I don't know so much these days. You tell me you're compromised. *Was this what we demanded of each other?* I tell you leaving a train is like getting your sea legs confiscated. You lend me yours. You have no use for them. We spend a weekend this way. I'm still years later. This is all past tense. I just don't know how to say that yet.

6. OBSOLESCENCE

Garner a body's worth of chariot burials & riding tack. Worship our ugly mirroring. A conversation is two horses headed away from each other at breakneck speed. In my mouth are the forelegs of a proud stallion & pebble beaches. You are gelding the miles. We don't talk. We don't talk. Just ride into the sunset & claim we lasted as long as we deserved. There is a calculation to all our together just as there is weight to all our alone. We made the city using each other's horse bodies & the groan of skin. Our palms are licked clean of cement, salt & sugar & we promise we will remember each other. The iron horse laments another poor attempt at City planning & doesn't correct us.

Decanonize

Nudes with trigger warnings, a decade of missed visits.
Bodies' prematurely-cremated-pugilist stance at the indignation
of having to forgive their immolation. Clandestine screenings
of DVD menus, maintenance of living standards
set by the committee of home held hostage by elevator jazz.
Language of lonely. Power of less. I find I'm inclined
to denial by committee. I accept delivery. Sign for something tangible
to replace the weight of my chest with the weight of someone else's,
if only for a moment. Murmur to the past that wears out my favourite skin
you can keep it.
Refuse a narrative of comfort, quote science fiction instead of theory.
>*Intrepid of the body - you hold something we all need. So,*
>*fuck me with the hand you wear your wedding ring on - I want to*
>*feel something; to know I cannot fathom my own temporary.*

I'm back to living careful. In doing pretty good impressions of islands,
we will come to the realisation that the Saint of Birds' body was abandoned
on saplings so their corpse would be hoisted by the forest.
Decanonize me. Depluralize my coping strategies.
Deglove the hand you hold mine in. Tell me
there is nothing about survival that was meant to be pretty,
yet here we are, wondrously ugly in our alive,
the beatification of our making it.
Call us holy,
we have earned it.

Collapser

Surrender is souring sheets & betraying beds. Acceptance is ~the undoing of treaties made to rest. Change is the whales suspended in the dark waiting like light bulbs hoping for breath. There is no benefit to me to remember anything accurately. All that's asked of you is knowing to not yield to the pitch & yaw of broken railways. I made you admit you did ask me to marry you even if you never really meant it. There is a comfort in what I was never supposed to have become. I have been dropped in the railroad iron sea. I find my lungs are waiting rooms. Fare evasion. Missed connections in backwater stations. I don't want to be remembered by how fast or how far I was going when I met someone. We owe ourselves dorsal truths even to the detriment of nostalgia. For all our speech impediment the whales are promising compensation for not guarding the seas from us. We are surfacing from the commute of sleep. Finding station announcements bellow deep their apologies for delays A plume of steam erupts from the water's edge, as another escape fails to materialise. The plaintive spinal song prevents significant locomotive decay. Torsion lapse. The generosity of immobilisation. The barnacle cursed trolley stops to offer us an easy way out. We find everything is too much but we seldom even asked for enough. All the broken bottles beholden to memorialising me as stained glass windows are on leaving trains, a bouquet of cancelled names, the worship of boy replacement orchids. I am cinematic proof of the Montparnasse derailment which people mistook for the real thing. You are evidence of the perils of flight in whale sightings. Whole migration seasons disappeared. Everyone recommends going missing to give reason to remain or at least to better frame how you remember someone. In the now terrible ocean, the loneliest whale calls out to something it doesn't know it heard & doesn't know how to talk to. The last train home is more missing than late. I long for being forgotten. Seeming is a dying narrative. Escape, the same as return, is fragile with potential.

Normalise Knife Fighting Your Therapist

Today the papers, in the West at least, are heavy with corrections. The body of the unidentified man washed up in Avonmouth was in fact a wasp nest set with rhinestone & pearl typewriter keys; the Bristol cryptids found stealing canopic jars were activists grown over by forests. In the flat above a fish & chip shop, in Keynsham, the river museum archivists have discovered a new species living in the exhibits rather than the biomes they represent. They won't speak of it. You dream sour. Waking up is revisionist propaganda that *no, it's always been this way*. The wind is leading the day to the type of danger you'd need a new god to navigate, but the schools are broken for the season & the motorways are a packed congregation of family worship praying for the sea. Escape is a kind of hope. I heard from reliable sources that you have been looking into mirrors in your dreams. You're telling yourself you can get through this again. But you can't. All the people found in mirrors are staging a tournament to appoint your successor. They line up in your reflection to see which one you most believe is you &, having access to your memories, they do a pretty good impression of you but also of being OK which you have never done so if you know what to look for it's easy to figure out who's real. You've been looking to prove you are real for so long now. I hear your dreams are the type in which your home gets bigger the longer you stay there. I hear you are dreaming of burning churches for getting the research wrong. I want you to wake up, I want you to stop being so scared. I don't know what's going on, but it can't be all that bad. The misreporting is a kind of myth building. Maybe there are temples to all the bodies we lost lining the A38. They just become so much scenery. Backdrop. Stendhal syndrome of context. In your dreams you & I are drawing Corsican Vendetta Stilettos to settle our differences. The biggest disparity is in our past. You are so intent on reclaiming it where I prefer to relive it. The papers having colluded with those paid to make sense of all our damage, confused reality with metaphor again & are recalcitrant of our history, redacting the part where they had us die & hoping instead, they start reporting how we lived.

Neptune's Daughter is a Lighthouse

I know you've yet to do a million things. Opening milk cartons searching for the boy you lost. Arranging sand grains by taste. Observing the wound of yesterday heal like scaffolding for having left it. But for now, let me take you to the mausoleum of rain. Museum of the flood. Exhibition of us. They've curated every artefact that would be destroyed by the tide to demonstrate what we stand to lose if we stay. My personal favourite is a diorama of us kept in the inside pocket of one of the jackets of one of the more senior guards. He's been working on it for years. We're remade in broken bone & papercut beneath a polystyrene night sky, peppered with empty constellations of shop brand cider. Our early attempts at immortality are captured in a kind, if factual, way. Be careful of your tongue - the custodians don't take well to any challenge of their sleepy archivism - they've a habit of erasure. They believe, perhaps rightly, we can't be trusted with our own history even before we make it. So we're not allowed to correct the monstrous, alabaster inaccuracies, but we can share a joke about how wrong they got it. You can flip through our younger superstitions with white gloves if you promise not to redact any of them. Acknowledge how any recollection is a chance to change. Any mythology is better than the one you believe in of yourself. Know that gods are poor replacements for history. There's space for them too but it's closed for cleaning today. Here in a Perspex box, with a tiny label that does no justice to the gravity of it, is the last moment we spoke. I've been signing petitions for the preservation of this reluctance. The label bears the reminder *"This donation is an inheritance."* But we knew that already. I found myself by starting at the last place I'd consider looking for me, focused on burning the marble white into ants. This was a moment of historic insignificance in that it was pre you & before I knew myself so pre me too. My hands are replete with legends that we both avoid correcting the attributions of. I will buy you a keepsake. A souvenir of revisionism. I promise this will be the last nostalgic diversion I ask you to take with me. A t-shirt that says, *"I too tried to evoke our history whilst avoiding the cruel knowledge of experience & all I got is this rose-tinted idealisation that hurt more than having never thought of it"*. It is a perfect fit. Even knowing no one else is allowed to see what we've seen, there's comfort in its existence. We can leave each other at the entrance, tip our pocket change to the gathered clouds & walk in opposite directions.

The Idea of Falling in Love in Vienna Is Propaganda

Overdrafts chewing on the exposed
red brick wound   of buildings   skinned by winter.
Transit talk, heart impediment speech bypass,

conversation starters for the terminally quiet.
The low scudding   of weather   beholden to roads.
That pervasive kind of sick that everyone is. Found

family memories gouged by profiteering.
We are blaming the parades   of boys becoming
butterflies for the chasms that held them. We glide

for want of closure to fucking hold us to something.
Permanence.   I can't.
Lungs are disputed territories. Boys caught exploding

become bibliographies. Only relevant now when cited in defensive
answering concerning leaving. Guarded first respondees.
The road signs mirror our loss. Time was, there used to be patron saints

for the missing. Our guilt complexes render us confessionals.
To be named paradox by sensory deprivation &
the foreign bodies the immune system sees us as.

I'm telling the walls I live in you're not to be trusted.
I'm holding my eyes in outstretched hands. I'm telling God what you said.
The most common cause of ascension

is these podiums caught in our torsos. Having choked
on every motel expectation demanded of me I want to be soft.
I want to not be alone & be treated with kindness.

Abstracts From a Dream City

…where some decadent jazz is playing & we are all soft lit winter drunk & in love. & our cherishing one another is somehow muted by the loud & the distance & the streets free from the wolf commute & the whale return. The city is a long exposure photograph of decay but in the most pleasing palette that, later, we will take our fill of - stuff stories into our sacred mouths & grin hamster cheeked at each other & pretend that here it's all ok. That the rotten world is only putting on a show of its demise for our benefit. The paracetamol of an early night spent *are you still thinking of me* pulls us together for a one-off reunion. The sleep logic of physics means our kisses & conversation are treacle punch slow, but we do mean them. I am sick with contracts. You are advocating for more accurate horizons. Both renegotiating for better sleep hygiene knowing it will mean we see each other less. Our school friends become contusions filled with butterflies, the ribcage staccato of punctuation & impenetrable walls like they always wanted to be. I am the swell of obscure film scores close to the denouement & you are a pavement of good intentions, credit scores & pragmatic relationships. Our eyes are piano keys, tentacles & all things hollow. We are heavy & bereft of flight but not so in love with gravity we can't leave. We are viewed in third person, to ensure the framing of us against pavement's perspective of capture, illuminated by amber's comfort, is how we will recall it. Your petrichor wife is rolling you awake, *rain, don't leave. Rain. wash me away.* Remember the reflected glow of our bodies on the slick streets of nostalgia. There's an overarching narrative of nostalgia even here lost to the cracks. Lost to collapse. Lost till we are found by the burden of waking.

Everyone I Have Ever Loved Is Getting Pregnant or Married or Fisted & That's Just Fine

You are becoming prone to grandiose testimonies in the second renaissance of us. Debating my right to be with tetchy linguistics deniers who only have a layman's grasp on quantum entanglement. These conspiracists are generous with history, planning as they are to renovate our house of hauntings. But you are an expert & I am only a weekend's worth of ghosts so why have me explain such nuance? Worship a shark god & they will make an ocean floor of you yet. Sinking cities beneath myth is a way to rewrite an insistence. The marble here is heinous in its revelry. Where once we believed, there is a desolate husband instead - returning the war he bought thinking you would love it. In all this argument we never considered the sternum, delegated the task of kissing to those least experienced. We promised it would work out; can you pass the message to our descendants that we lied. Someone masturbates but is not the speaker of this poem. You are clutching concrete bottle mapping – squeezing rebar from your history hoping the architecture not hold – I am smiling politely making promises rather than conversation. Disbelief is a large part of our lives these days – we press phatic the dry socket of a mouth's loss, orchids bloom from boys, & I am up to my elbows in foreign objects removed from dislocated bodies. We are unlearning patterns of flight & nurturing the dark whilst being unable to think of the coherence of all the tailbacks this kind of grieving leads to. You are the red & white of 80's Italian Restaurant tablecloths. I am the waiters in the alley out back sneaking a prayer between late shifts – we touch the prayer to each other's mouths, hungry for a burden though we are. Admire the discarded torsos of sentimental archivists – those go to our mouths too. The channelling of all that ungrowth we did to forget this loss. This too is a prayer. You talk of oral fixation & never acknowledge your mother problems; the breathing apparatus of kindness; or even the freediving when people never give you what you need. How your favourite pop stars are citing dream theorems on calculus in papers regarding the fall of Math in protest. You wouldn't want it if the logic held. Besides – if all you have is your mouth & your words it makes sense we do this much talk worship, familiarising ourselves with the towns we left, waxing nostalgic of the people we met at our worse, finding the gardens in the ugly of us & laying out blueprints for everything wrong with living & its causes. I am searching for very specific pornography hoping I might find out where we went wrong. I heard someone call you a celebrity of the worst kind of rubbernecking. I hope you stay to watch me burn. Worship whatever you need to. I'll stick with you. Pray a mouth with me, hungry your ear. Lord knows I have a need of the kind of mercy you are created for.

Debridation

Beholden   to traditions of salting wounds on anniversaries, I become
something   of an expert on both techniques to prolong life
expectancy & on   drowning. I am starting to cultivate bone in
place of memories. To develop   flood defences rather than coping
strategies. To allow all the lies I tell   myself to keep the sea at bay
to take root. I'm hoping it will save us, knowing   it won't. I have
gained a taste for the measuring of grief - a tongue whose   wound I
am fluent in. I am fraught with knowledge. Beset by information.
Burdened by forgetting. I wasn't to know there'd be a time I would wish to
be overwhelmed. Observing the remnants of sowing season peels back
the day from its wreckage there's no reason for the limits we   place on
ourselves hoping to be better than we are. No reason   the sea should
grow though we planted it in our torsos   hoping to become islands.
No reason our last monument to   forgetting has become something
of a celebrity in my   absence. But it has. So we proselytise the
notion   our   history should dictate how we act in context of those
to   come   after. It's an assurance we tell the grieving I have little time for.

Rose Tinted Fresnel Lens Objecting to a Still Life of Sunlight in a Living Bedroom, September 2016

Driftwood floors caught in the current of a Saint Werburgh's September
yield calloused bodies monastic, maintaining composure though sinking.
      You were more than enough.
Bosun of the golden hour, how your hair was so red.
Building bridges between skin and finding vulnerable the taste of breath
      - you learn to hold yourself.
Wind wounded bodies and all that thinking
ourselves abhorrent that tried to force our hands, the crab touch
of exoskeleton handwriting. We have both been hurt beaching
on yet another lonely fractal wetland. I promise I'll not leave
the remnants of my worry regalia for you to abdicate
the losing sea. I find your coast, I promise to keep this moment
and I do. Years from now, you happy and free
caring despite my violent disbelief in me, you tell me
I saved you from yourself. This reads like an embassy
to lost boys, but I know your many pillowed bed
is an outreach programme for sleep. The carefully strewn
patchwork counterpanes quell fugue states and you had me read you
stories in bed. Your words are a grief-stricken jazz band,
little mouse in a lonely bar, play your sad circus music.
Your hands wallowed a lonely dirge, clear my body
of all promontories waiting crash. If we had made it
to shore so certain of our own navigation I'd not be so thankful
we had each other. Not be at a good enough vantage point
to see how even in the absence of my sinking,
how glad I am that you're better now.

Zuiyo-Maru Carcass Remembering

Two mothers let their girls play in motorways
I get it. The cars are family to traffic
& the edging of human sacrifice is a coping mechanism
so this makes sense in a sibling kind of way.
Grieving is the opposite of touching & we're simple engines of brute force &
moving on. Hooked on this kind of Cotard delusion where instead
of being dead everyone you love is a Rube-Goldberg machine.

Madame, your children are throwing roses
yet yesterday they unveiled a great whale carcass
colossal with pig grief. I'm not angry
but I want to ask how they got it here
when it was exactly what I needed.

You stormed the party as an unexpected contender
at the dead bodies Oscar's. The red carpet loves you
sticky with blood as it is. The children who studied
at the church of the scientific method have asked you
not abandon them in their time of need - to be a guarantor for their impartiality.
I am here in theory only, downing litre after litre of medical grade kerosene.
No internal organs but my jaws and spine, remain somehow intact.

Madame! These roses, do you need them returned?
I need a bouquet for stopping journeys
As bloated with complex ecosystems as I.
Glass shard brittle worms, sleeper sharks
& the empty of a life sunk. My friend was alive once,
you have helped me understand how now he is not.

Season of Rust

& we are eating pastries in the easy sunshine of a brisk March morning
& you are fat & alive & here & thinking of ordering another coffee &
considering going vegan in a empty bedroom kind of way & we are catching
up & you are smiling a newspaper kind of smile, & we are discussing later,
both tacitly avoiding the knowledge there is no later, but you are here &
hopesong & harmless & now & i don't mind that my housemate leaves the
bathroom too loud to not disturb us because if i spent much longer here with
you, i too, like you, would not have wanted to return, but i made a promise in
your absence that i would never leave those already left behind so i do not.[1]

---

1. instead chide myself for the rejection of such small luxuries. I,
like everyone else, never have time to acknowledge the damage of
refusing so I ignore my own ignoring, hope to tighten my belt as the years
swell. Sometimes, there's a necessity in forgetting the cruelty the past has
taught us. I've taken to negotiating with the birds - they will cherish & honour
me & name me in their anatomy giveaway programmes & i'm to stop asking
they send messages to you. I am always waiting for the chorus of a homesick
March to spill onto the pavement for the first good of the year & we will catch
up & share pastries, & both demand the other tells us everything first.

Desolation Rituals

It was starvation time at the need museum & we were doing our best. Bodies offered skin respite & we were doing a lacklustre impression of together. It was November, cold with archives, & the insolence fucked gape of our honest mouths yearned for better days. The scale of all our loss truly awed us. Interrupting our divorce proceedings, a former Trustee of the Corpses called, offering guided tours of incisions I never healed from. I had been too scared of being forgotten to screen their calls. You were already too oil painted into the walls of this institution to deny my curiosity, with your canvas skin demanding voyeurism. I know you won't be worried about me much longer. The relics left in our lungs by this conversation will be misinterpreted. I am the Parthenon Selene Horse collapsing, tombstone printed dialogue & preservation rituals. History kept that way.

I tell them
A body can be left to science but not to art & I have incisions in my pockets to ensure thrifty spending. To keep my hands from running their empty mouths at all the distance not recorded in this stupid gallery. This graven year. This GP appointment queue of a life. This month of meal deals fucked budgeting.

They respond that I
am a legacy that deserves to be returned.
So, I return, cut you soft from your gilt frame & apologise for the longing. We call this vandalism but can't bear to codify ourselves. Claim our history doesn't own us. We wanted to see the interactive cadaver exhibition, but departure is a privilege. The souvenirs of Sanctuary. You are bearing the deterioration scars of framing & restorationists are cynical about returning you to your former condition. The customer satisfaction survey waiting at the exit was just the curator hanging, priapic hoping for recognition. We kissed him & thanked him for the experience but left before he made us a donation. We don't realise it but we, like him, will one day spend our time masturbating over the exhibit of what was. This stupid dance of being human. This body thirsting surveillance. This nostalgia cunted grief.

Guild of Thirst

A half hour of alarms; riverdreaming early
warning system: a moment of comfort denied
not yet, no one wants to become Dredge, awake, haul gone
the silt of lungs. Bend if the oxbow lake wills it so.
Can you graduate from grief? Truly wield the expertise of doubt?
The margins are where erosion hits hardest.
There is a morning where they are not missing
but the sea follows with the years when they are.
A moment lasts as long as a stickleback tongue
does not relent its miserly glory nor the wishbones found
flourishing in the glut
of remaining. Tiny prayer to the fear
of drowning. Acknowledging the guild of thirst collects dues
it isn't owed. The indignant protests of floods wash away
the forests of throats whose roots hold our form.
How pliable the river and unasked of, the mouth.
How quiet the demands of floodplains willing themselves to stop.

///Castle.quiet.speeds

Having never had need
to ever build refuge
we make do
with the river silent arch
of the old copper works
found on a wet walk.
A sanctuary kept quiet
from all valley ensembles singing
their storm & the bureaucracies of loving.
Hindsight is a demanding place to live in
so we only visit, mention the past in passing
Museum of the lesson. Relinquishing
our history. Disarticulating
our memories. Empty of time,
open to the terms of surrender
if not the loss
Tender is the night
for refusing. Excessive
the hill with falling. Scarce
the ground with landing.
Long & lonely, my arms
with empty. Open
is the wound
that allows itself relenting.
Inchoate with yearning
is my body & scared again.

Poem in Which My Ex's New Partner Approaches Me to Help Them Write Marriage Vows.

Sexy slenderman gangbanged in abandoned hospitals by father figures
I ejaculate loudly in an empty home
amateur condemned houses (POV) in interracial fucking
I switch my longing to guilt mode & mea culpa my sorrys for objectification
post-apocalyptic conjoined redhead twins stuck in a fridge.
this time I really mean it, my post nut clarity wins the Palme d'or
mirror twinks, slowly peel back the skin from their bones as the other gets his
guts sucked from his body by amateur pool filter.
the following day I'm stuck in traffic
echo of dead friends trapped in student debt solo size queen squirt fest
ahead a grisly accident I cannot possibly fantasise about
brutalist architecture defunded by police (roleplay)
even knowing it's a thick hot 18-wheeler & a MILF in a people carrier.
stepbrother apologising for the trauma caused in childhood
coming to my senses I mourn the wound the world made of my body
genuinely in love couple captured on SECRET cams sewn into their skin
I hear sharks have been sighted off the street we said we'd live on.
forced to watch - exes holding hands with each other & laughing
the truth is worse, it wasn't their new partner but them
everyone I have ever loved is getting creampied or pregnant or fisted or loved
unconditionally or married or having their ass eaten or loved in the way they
deserve by someone I could never be & that's just fine
You're doing better now, where I'm caught wondering if bodies define holding
hand holding with a short northern girl (ASMR)
I lose myself to horizons, select a fresh tragedy to wank over
you calling me by my name
I am searching for you in unwanted places. I won't be surprised when this
repeats itself.

Mistaking Closure Sex for Reconciliation Sex

We're fucking! In the years of loss we have left & come back with
other people's body parts & the architecture of our chests changes to
accommodate fresh perspectives. In the moments of clarity, you ask gently
if you can absolve yourself completely & curl into my body. In the after,
having harvested our need, we will agree to swap spit but demand back the
missing weeks & so it will never last. We're fucking! The difference between
holding onto headboards or interlocking our fingers, this is a prayer our
mouths make for the missing churches our legs become - tessellating in the
most nostalgic of puzzles of absent congregations. We're fucking & this is a
crossover episode where everyone has to play the part. Unwittingly inviting
our history into our skin. Uncovering archaeology of us. Unveiling each
other's bones & pirouettes. There's a studio audience. They're marvelling at
the stunt work. Body doubles committed to becoming mountains. We're
fucking! Both needing to be filled. We're fucking. Waiting eagerly for the
fall of empires despite all our momentary telling me this time it won't
come. We're fucking, we're fucking! we're fucking; we're fucking & you're
telling me I need to forgive myself we're fucking? But it's complicated. No!
We're fucking with gravity; composure; & the salt of our language making
tender work of falling then pulling out of that particular ego death. We're
fucking with gravity watching. We're helping universal constants explore
their marriage. Strong force & time are in bed with us. We are fucking. We
are making space for ourselves in the corridors of each other. We are asking
for a moment to sluice our throats with ice water. We are making treaties
to the embassies of our want. We are. We are. We are. We are post coital,
touching tender debating if gravity is a god. We're fucking! You are talking
of prostate milking, leather & not feeling like you can breathe except when
being choked. There is stubble rash on your chin & thigh. You are smiling in
the exact language of missing. You are asking kindly & showing very clearly
exactly how you liked to be touched now & time is so fucking impatient.

We're fucking. On & off. We are asking each other for a break & to switch positions. You be the cage & I be the capture. You be the stage & I'll be the actor. You be certain & I'll be the fracture. We're fucking. Wristwork at the ready. We're fucking. SSRIs telling me we really need to figure out what this is beyond the immediate. We're fucking. Telling me you love what I represent. Telling me that we are fucking if only we knew what that meant anymore & asking with our bodies if this distance can tender two years' worth of unmade beds & empty windows. We're fucking. You are asking me if there's gravity from all this closure & I am complaining about all that needing damage & the unwritten ritual of our hands. We're wearing our old skin. We are fucking - bodies full of bite templates, yielding to familiarity. We're hoping for some form of revelation. We're fucking. We're fucking. But then you apologise for getting carried away & say it was a force of habit. We're fucking. Say it was a lapse. We're fucking. Say it was only temporary. These things so often are. We're fucking & it's not that these things hurt more or less this long after, just that I never allowed myself to feel then when I should have done. We are fucking & trying to find respite from how after so long our bodies simply lose the shorthand of empty. We are fucking & trying not to cry. You are clasping my ears to the side of my head, looking right in my eyes & yelling something indecipherable but knowing your predilection for ownership & never letting go of the dead boy I became I think you are saying *you are loved you are loved you are loved & all of this doesn't matter because you are mine, you are mine, you are mine*

You Became the Entire Circus, Surprised at Getting Creampied by Clowns

so, the roadside attractions & haunted houses of your body
have finally admitted they never recognised you.
So what. So desolate & so underfucked & so jumping-in-the-coffin
of-every-funeral-you-attend as you are, this should come as little surprise.
Everyone's been crowding into graves; it seems you've missed your shot.
There's nothing under any cups that empty themselves as you do,
there's no reflection left that looks like you,
the howl is all that's left of the lion now you've tamed yourself.
The man hungry for swords cannot withstand another peace process.
The freak show's full & even you can admit they wouldn't welcome you
not ever, ever having lasted longer than widespread legs & bodies waiting
for big tops. Maybe others have developed better sideshows to keep them
distracted. But you have a crowd hunger that won't divulge
the disappearing act of mobs to strangers. You have a hand's worth
of history yearning for daredevils & running off to join whatever
latest idea will have you. But nostalgia tourists won't linger in the milk
of a candy floss sticky day & expect anything
more than a handful of tickets. Everyone was talking
behind your back in the hall of mirrors. The uncanny valley
of compacting a crowd's worth of grief into a beat-up car
that would never stop for hitchers looking like you.
Still performing the stunt work of attrition
you wreck your decadence tongue grease painting
the rumour of another day, a lathe of brief wonder.
An obsession queuing for cheap tricks. Your calliope chest collapses
as you admit you never wanted anything more than laughter,
the applause of personhood. The last wet chance
of throwing knives cloying for skin.

Simulating Wound Healing From a Growth Perspective

Scorpio-moon-corduroy-skin of a wrecked childhood. Vanilla paper aeroplanes. Bodies as flight plans, bodies as pleurisy of birds trapped in walls & the songs they sing to keep themselves aloft. Everything we were unsure of. Sycamore narratives & the choke hold flower by Kenzo had on me. I'm sorry you were so considerate.

I wish there had been something to save us rather than each other.

We devoured the buoyancy from the inside of our cheeks. Kept our aeronautics to ourselves. Made certain none of the wings lining our chest made their way into the real. Argued it does not matter how we lived, just that we did.

I kept an inventory of what was offered me in your absence. Front seat passenger rites: airways, dismantled & talk-therapy concrete-throats. Poor replacement for you but all I am deserving of. Our Wrigley's spearmint laden voices kept flight secrets from the fall of our bodies, left hollow bones fluent in gift shop memories.

Years later, I'm pulling wishbones from my dreams. People still stop & ask me where the rest of me is. I don't tell them about the osteotomies that keep me from flying. I don't ask them as I would you -Throatbird, lull your song into me & apologise for colonising my body. It's too long to keep grieving the clipped wing of a boy missing the gastrolith & lore from his skin. But the waxwings & grackles & orioles begging their autonomy from our lungs are what defined us.

Our bodies are black box recorders for a childhood that was never designed to be gotten out of alive. I'm a husk of man, birdless & still wondering why I can't fly. I have little remaining to me but blurry pictures I can't bear to look at & a history in Aviation English I can't parse to civilians. I salvaged it all anyway, the bruise receipts; micro dosing contact; the avian kingdom of excuses; quiet fire; the parallels of tomato hearts; & wrists - tourmaline soft; even the conversations about dead friends. I kept it all. So help me but I had to.

Inside You Are Two Wolves, One Is Gay the Other Doesn't Know How to Tell You Your Heart Is Badly Built Bridge

Yesterday has voted on reintroducing glass wolves to shatter our Midwest torsos. Baby, this time I won't blink. We were both unaware that hindsight is a democracy. But with remembering demanding more from us than repetition - we're working on bettering ourselves whilst the world burns. We're servicing ourselves with the owner's manual from the fridge we insisted would save our marriage. Agreeing not to adopt wolves from cinema walls so our home won't get repossessed by tornadoes. Baby, we're nothing but retrospect. The government guidelines concerning the taming of the wilds are oblique & full of prairie talk. From what I gather we're expected to be fully licensed & registered before we attempt to capture the feral highways beneath our tongues. I am meeting cactus

men in dusty public bathrooms to discuss the philosophy of masculinity. You are idly masturbating for strangers on the internet & signing petitions with no regard for your personal data. You are saving the whales. You almost have the whole collection. We call this love & it almost is. The guidelines given us are looking more like demands. The guidelines are encroaching on our understanding of intimacy. The guidelines are starting to look more like cages. Apparently, if a wolf were to ever make it back to the bone sea, & haul the candid nature of its own undoing with it, then the entire rehabilitation is done over from scratch. Apparently, a wolf is just as likely to surrender as it is to remember. Apparently, as far as history has been recorded, this is the way it has always been. I cannot tell your declarations of love apart from their propaganda so I tell you all the ravine & sunset ways I cherish you whilst reading the fine print. Baby, I am so proud of all the distance you're accomplished. You swear to me that we can keep it together if we just believe it. You always did have a way of convincing me. You promise that the metaphysics of our suburban decor won't be negated by conservation efforts. That if we begin again, it will be different. Our tongues meet on the gum Arabic sealing divorce proceedings - this is where we are glad we have learned enough about each other to not forget it if we tried. Baby, I'm glad we tried. The wolves are taking online courses to learn how doors work. The wolves are calling us scabs for breaking the union. The wolves are furious awaiting rebates to better spend their feral. The wilderness is making amends to the lost again. We are told to be thankful that our taxes are going some way to making it unliveable. That we should all shoulder a portion of blame. The rehabilitation will be pronounced a resounding success whilst we are forgetting how to say our names. We shall sheathe our canines in failures' bodies, commit to remaining unknown & become South for the winter.

No Better a Cathedral Than a Body

Ritual held against sweat small backs
in the glut of summer
beneath altar cloth. I'll find the choir
in the dark yield. If I speak to you in sign, is it still a prayer
or is the evidence less reverent to the faith that we will make it?
If I wield an applause inside the holy of you,
will you walk alive through Heaven's doors, translating
the body to something even god can't pretend they don't understand?
Will you appreciate the patience we place on our tongues -
replacements for sleep song? Heart sick bodies & their medicine.
We have stopped resisting the hunger, our churches to need.
Between us the *Che vuo* is a rhetorical question. You confess,
you don't remember the first time you laid awake glistening
at the possibility of a god. You don't remember you could be held
in reverence by sacrament, demand, & the great divide.
There is a feud of bereavement knowing it is momentary.
I'll pray the night with you.
Believe whatever apostasy
you need of me.

And You

And you've gone vegan now which is understandable since you have lived in the city so long and you never really enjoyed the morning pastries I cherished. And a year is a terrible thing and you have known others, and so have I and you have moved to your own place that I never seen the inside of, and you still know my address and my routines and you say you're sleeping better now and I say I'm sorry it took such a hellish year to get you the help we all deserve. And you are a voice I still slip into in the cold hours and yours is a joke I still share with my friends, and I picked up a book called the psychology of romantic love, and it never once talks of feeling trapped and so I still don't have answers for you. And you are older now and I am too. And you are a part of me I wouldn't wish to relent, and we have a history but it's the constant renewing of shark's teeth on sword handle skin. And you say we want different things and never tell me what they are so I can protest and promise and swear that I want them too and maybe you're right and I just never realised it was pity not closure you were offering. And I'm still found looking for you in places I could not bear to see you in, and you are still in my dreams as a voice of the true North. And all we have is horror and the deadening soft of nostalgia and you are much further away but still too close to bear. But maybe it's better this way.

When You Wake Up You Will Be Whole

How few the history of us
& tentative the possibility.
How greater the wound for its brevity
& singularly unexplored the chance
How deep the grief
& unsettled the damage.
How patient the absent for waking
& how long the sleeper for their denying.
How I protected myself from the hurt
& opened the missing wider for having abandoned it.

I Was at the Conference for Your Former Lovers and Not One of Your Exes Knew You...

...but they all commented on how kind you were, all mentioned how
gentle you are, how soft your eyes and patient your touch. They all wore
badges bearing their name and dates and they all have questionnaires to
fill in and compare notes with and they laugh when they see how mostly
close they are and sometimes it's shock at how long between them and the
next there is and some never really knew you and some thought they did
but can't match up their history with yours and they grieve you again, like
they did back then and take turns to remember their favourite memory of
you. Distance has a tendency to fonder hearts. We can see by looking back.
Light grows weary with long. So the current understanding is that redshift
gives all things looked back on a rose tint. So no one mentions your small
cruelties. How not letting them was a pyrrhic defence. How you could
grow cold if you thought anyone was trying to know you better than you
let them. One takes the sunset you shared and says "this was true at least"
another, a professional addict counsellor now, shares all the small gifts and
acts of service and says "*no one since has been like th*is" another was glad that
you took the time out of your life long after it was over to sour the memory
of yourself by calling up at confessing your love two years after the fact and
the others all nodded in agreement. One who only had a day pass says they
would never have wished for anything but the best for you if only you had
let them. Not one of them had ever heard forever from you but all admitted
you had a heart bigger than your stomach. Greedy for it all, never knowing
what would happen. There were no keynote speakers at the conference.
All your exes shared pictures of their families and the lives they had lived
without you and promised to stay in touch but never did.

Wound Detail

I have been kept awake wondering if accent is defined by body
whilst kissing like divorcees. Basking sharks, irreparable
fractures & oil slick cormorants have all been sighted
off the street we once said we would live on. Knowing others
may offer you better dreaming patterns is a kingdom of want
lost to the flood. I loved you in the wake of seas claiming the land.
When you dragged me to yet another addict festival,
the three beautiful daughters of the doctor whose life we ruined
arranged to renovate our dream home in our absence. They claimed
it was recompense for the malpractice of our bodies becoming anchors.
For their father who told us we could not breathe underwater.
For the refusal of history to relent its closure. I crave this
generous a revenge for all my unrequited drownings. But still want to
shallow our graves to protest this misdiagnosis, calm the chest of its horses
 & give in to the indulgence of mapping skin. Instead, I wreck
the sleep of history with context. Sour torsos with longing &
set unsustainable precedents for coastline paradoxes like us.
My ribs are revetments guarding my heart against scour. The scar isn't fluent
in the tide's dialect. Everything we built refuses to believe
in its own collapse & craves to be unburdened by sleep & mourning
one another & in our absence, develops a fear of drowning.

I Don't Want to Love You Anymore...

…don't want to think about us. Don't want to remember how your skin tastes,
body looks in the dark, voice sounds in the small. I don't want
to know the North of you anymore - possibilities are the body's way of saying
"I'm no longer deserving of the places you once held for me "
Forgetting must be easier but I am loathe to relinquish the keys. I don't want
apartment complex bodies gentrifying my head to make hollow spaces
for pine journalists to document our movement; could I ever have been enough?
The rented circumstance of a floorplan - my wanting you to fight for me,
the sofa reupholstered & sickened by voices. I don't want to be found
in a home of blunt asking; two sour years of vanishing & the neglect
of demographic displacement; homes obscene with your not being here.
I don't want to acknowledge I never gave this the chance it deserved. I don't want
to admit my leaving left me open for a you that would not return. I don't want
to learn to separate what you represent with what you actually were. I don't want
to know how the clutter of living is so very different from the wild of abandoned.
I don't want to be so familiar with empty. I don't want to say goodbye. I don't want
for this to have ended, to have to be alone again, for this be over. I don't want
to be haunted by regulations & contracts telling me how
I was meant to have held the weight of your caring. I don't want
to suffer the planning permission of burnt bridges but I loved you too long now -
arms trying to hold onto all of these things like a horizon holds the city.
I didn't know what to do with everything you offered me when you did.
But now, given nothing, my home is fluent in the feral
language of absence. Speaking a tongue I don't want.

Acknowledgements

Errors of the Human body appeared in Acropolis Journal Issue 71, *Debridation* was published by Fawn Press in The Elements Issue as *Learning to Run With Scissors*. *Desolation Rituals* appeared in Graphic Violence Lit as *Slow Decomposition for an Extant Virtue*. *Mistaking Closure Sex for Reconciliation Sex* was published in Sweet Tooth and *Zuiyo Maru Carcass Remembering* was featured on IAMB Poetry.

With immense thanks to Aaron & the Broken Sleep Team for putting their trust in this work & unending thanks to Flick who got me into writing & anyone who has ever loved me & was so fucking patient with me.

LAY OUT YOUR UNREST

www.ingramcontent.com/pod-product-compliance
Lightning Source LLC
Chambersburg PA
CBHW051740040426
42447CB00008B/1232